SH 344

MW01156732

MARK KNOPFLER
GET LUCKY

Published by
Wise Publications
14-15 Berners Street,
London W1T 3LJ,
United Kingdom.

Exclusive distributors:
Music Sales Limited
Distribution Centre,
Newmarket Road, Bury St Edmunds,
Suffolk, IP33 3YB, United Kingdom.

Music Sales Pty Limited
20 Resolution Drive, Caringbah,
NSW 2229, Australia.

DG70950
ISBN 978-1-84938-271-7

This book © Copyright 2009
Wise Publications, a division
of Music Sales Limited.

Edited by Tom Farncombe.
Music arranged by Matt Cowe.
Music processed by Paul Ewers Music Design.
Original CD package design by Salvador Design.

Printed in the EU.

www.musicsales.com

WISE PUBLICATIONS
PART OF THE MUSIC SALES GROUP
London / New York / Paris / Sydney / Copenhagen / Berlin / Madrid / Tokyo

BORDER REIVER

Words & Music by Mark Knopfler

†Symbols in parentheses represent names with respect to capoed guitar.
Symbols above represent actual sounding chords. (Tab 0 = 1 fr.).

HARD SHOULDER

Words & Music by Mark Knopfler

slip road,

got a slipped load

and it's a hard _____ shoul - der to

sound as a pound,   right as rain –   right   as   rain.

Instrumental chorus

And it's a hard_____ shoul-der to cry on –

to cry on.

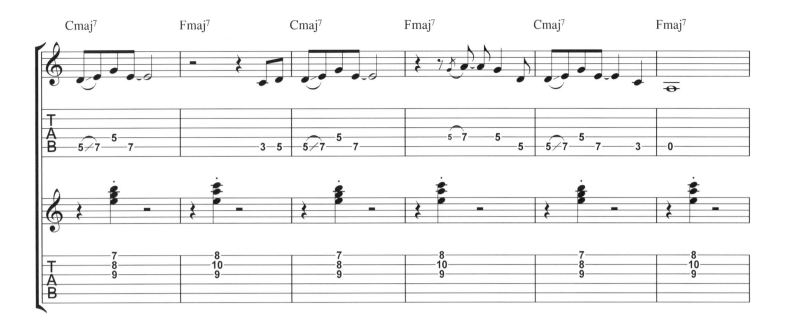

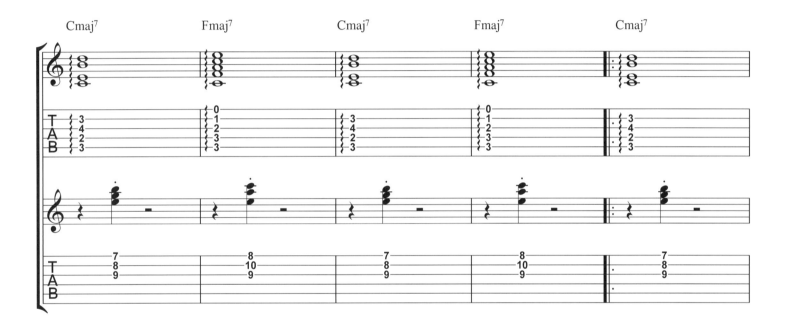

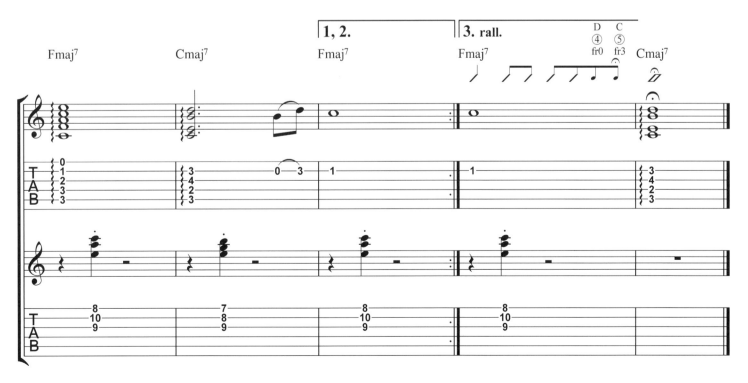

YOU CAN'T BEAT THE HOUSE

Words & Music by Mark Knopfler

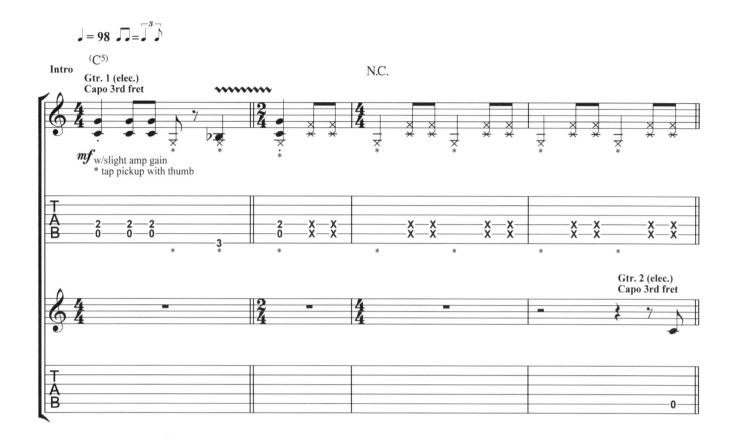

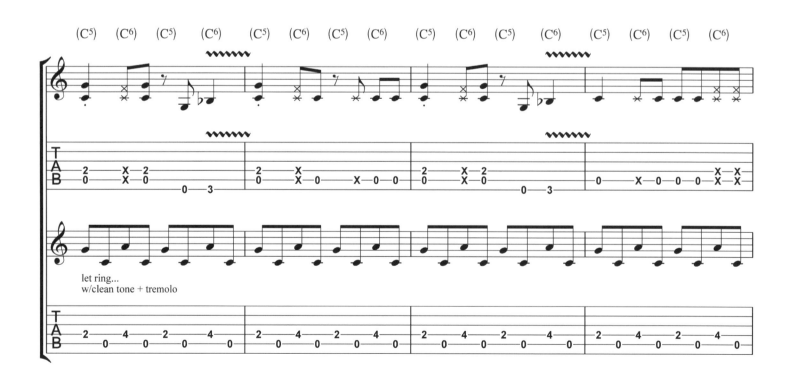

Bridge

You want to buy you a dance,__ don't buy it in here. It's all skin games and jel - ly roll,

red - eye and beer. (They're) all as mean as rat__ snakes, all got knives__ in their boots.

BEFORE GAS & TV

Words & Music by Mark Knopfler

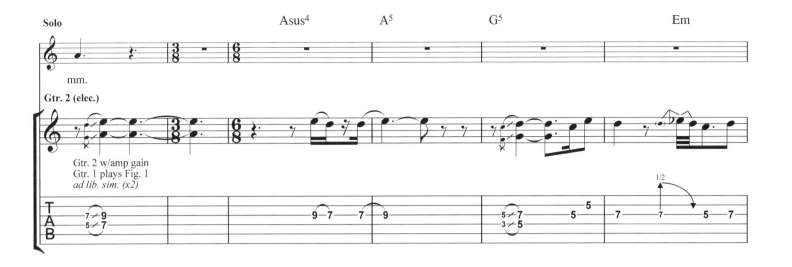

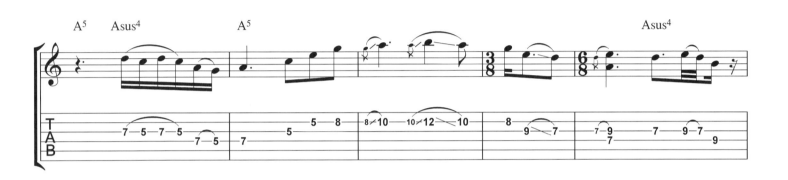

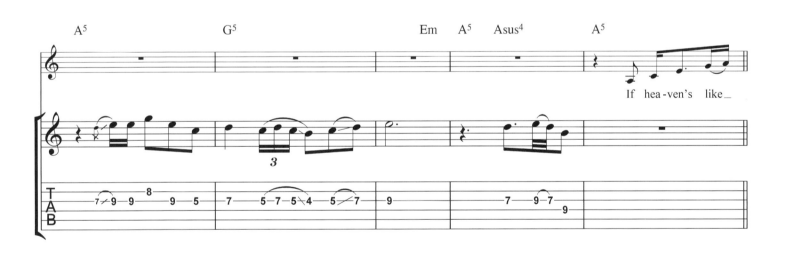

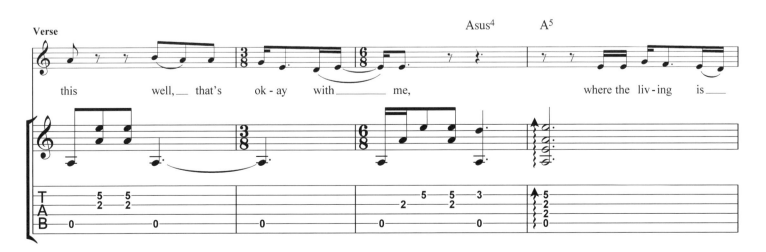

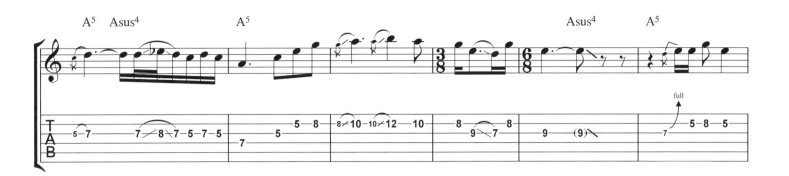
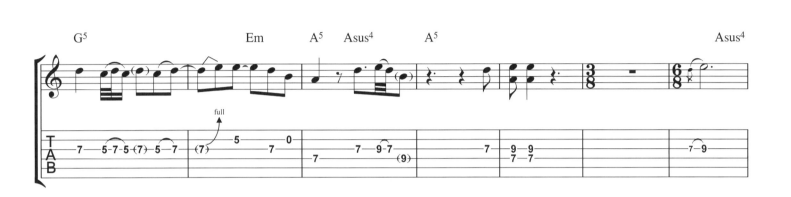

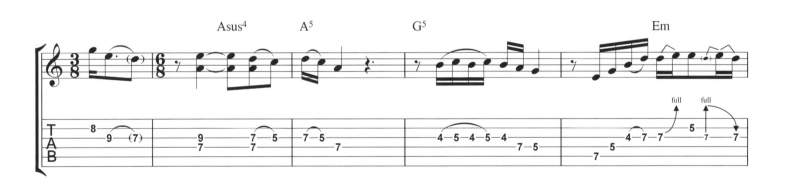
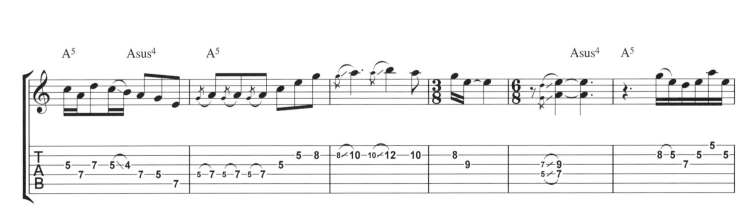

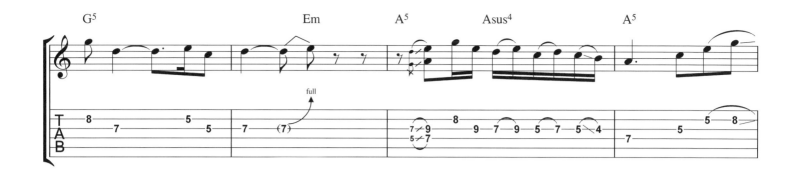

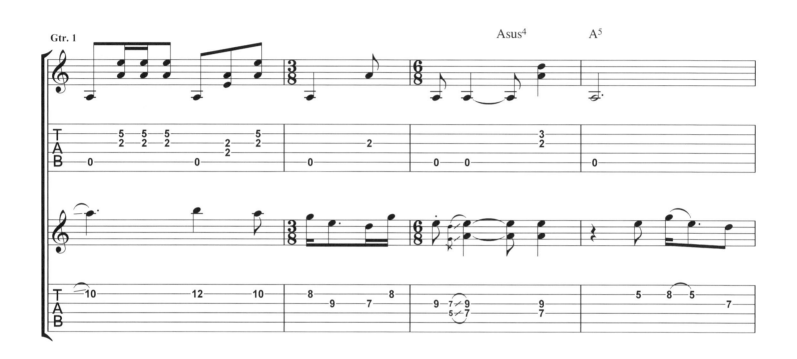

MONTELEONE

Words & Music by Mark Knopfler

Capo 2nd fret

†Symbols in parentheses represent names with respect to capoed guitar.
Symbols above represent actual sounding chords. (Tab 0 = 2 fr.).

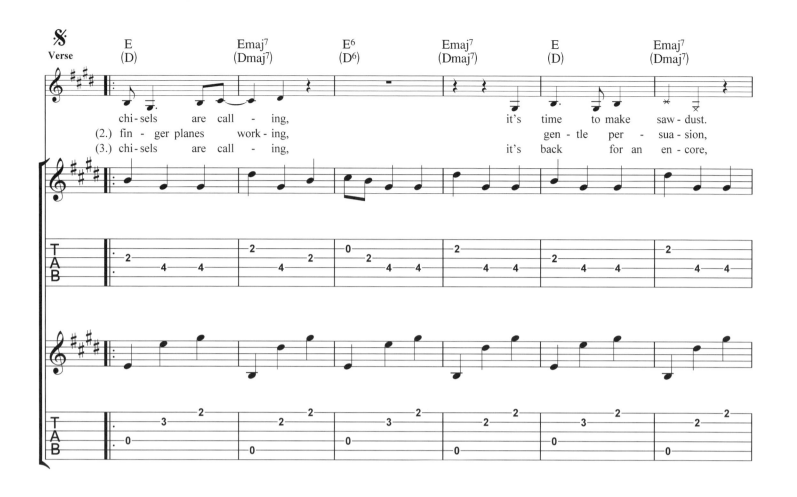

chi-sels are call - ing, it's time to make saw - dust.
(2.) fin - ger planes work - ing, gen - tle per - sua - sion,
(3.) chi-sels are call - ing, it's back for an en - core,

Steel - y re - mind - ers of things__ left to do,__
I bend to the wood__ and I coax it to sing.__
back to the shav - ings that cov - er the floor.__

Mon - te - le - o - ne, a man - do - lin's wait - ing for you.
Mon - te - le - o - ne, your new one and on - ly will ring.
Mon - te - le - o - ne, a call for more.

(2.) My

Mon - te - le - o - ne, your
Mon - te - le - o - ne,

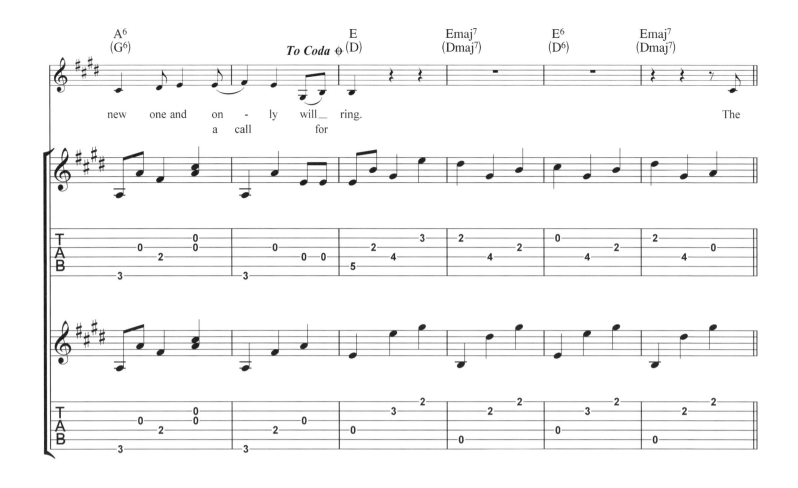

new one and on - ly will ring.
a call for

The

rain on the win - dow, the snow on the gra - vel, the sea - sons go by to the songs

in the wood. Too quick or too care - less it all could un - rav - el,

it so eas - 'ly could.

Solo

D.S. al Coda

3. The

Coda

Strings cue

more.

37

CLEANING MY GUN

Words & Music by Mark Knopfler

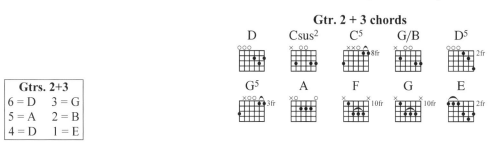

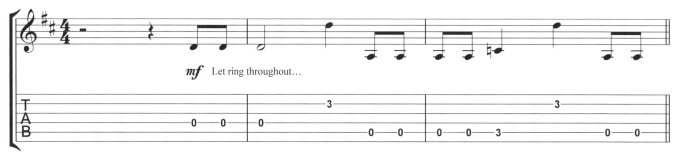

To match original recording, tune all guitars down 1 semitone

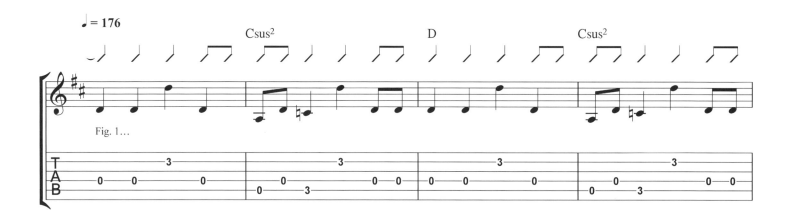

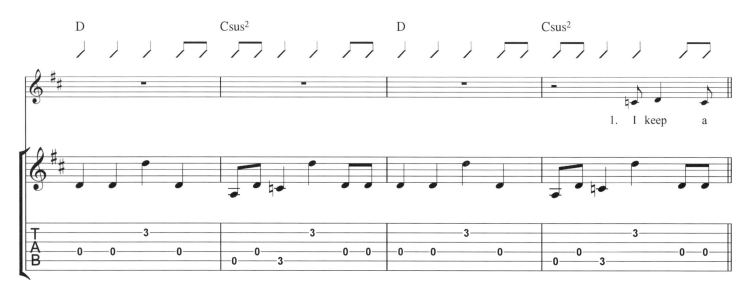

I'm not com - plain - ing, it's the world___ we live in.

...Fig. 1 ends

2. Blar - ney and Ma - lar - key, they're a de - vi - ous firm,___
3. Re - mem - ber it got___ so cold___ ice___ froze up the tank,___
4. gave you a ma - gic bul - let on a lit - tle chain

Gtr. 3 (elec.)

Gtr. 3 w/amp gain
Gtr. 1 plays Fig. 1

2° Gtr. 3

3° Gtr. 3

we hired theworst   dish - wash - er   this place   ev - er got.
case   of   Old__ Dam - na - tion   for when   you get   here,__ my   friend.
an - y   which   way,   we're gon - na   need   a lit - tle   luck.

(3°) You   can

Come in be - low the ra - dar,   they want to spoil our _____ fun, ___
We can have our - selves a _____ par - ty ___   be - fore they _____ come, ___
still get gas in Hea - ven,   and a drink in King - dom

Solo

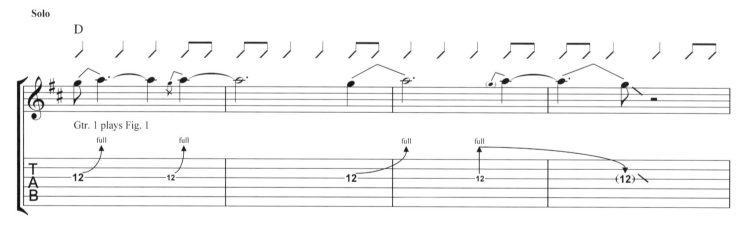

Gtr. 1 plays Fig. 1

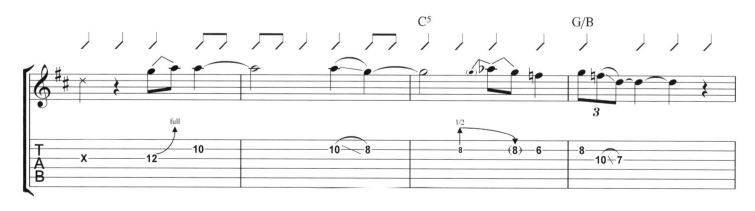

We had wo-men and a mir-ror ball, we had a dee jay,

Gtr. 1

47

used to eat   pret - ty much   all   that   came_   his   way._____

Ev - er since   the   goons___   came in___   and took a - part__   the place,___

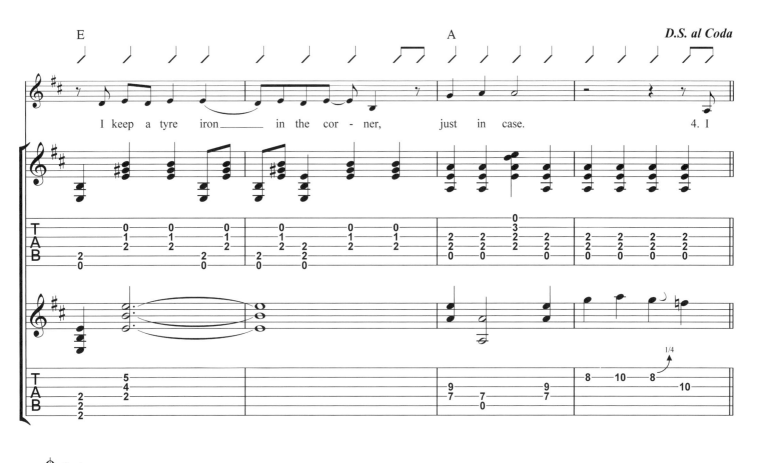

I keep a tyre iron_____ in the cor - ner, just in case. 4. I

gun._____

Fig. 2 - Gtr. 1 plays Fig. 2 *ad lib. sim. (x15)*

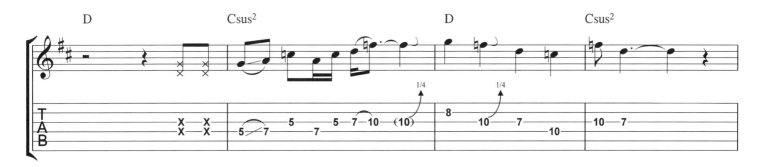

THE CAR WAS THE ONE

Words & Music by Mark Knopfler

54

The lyrics visible in the sheet music: "The car__ was the one," and "the car__ was the one."

REMEMBRANCE DAY

Words & Music by Mark Knopfler

†Symbols in parentheses represent names with respect to capoed guitar.
Symbols above represent actual sounding chords. (Tab 0 = 2 fr.).

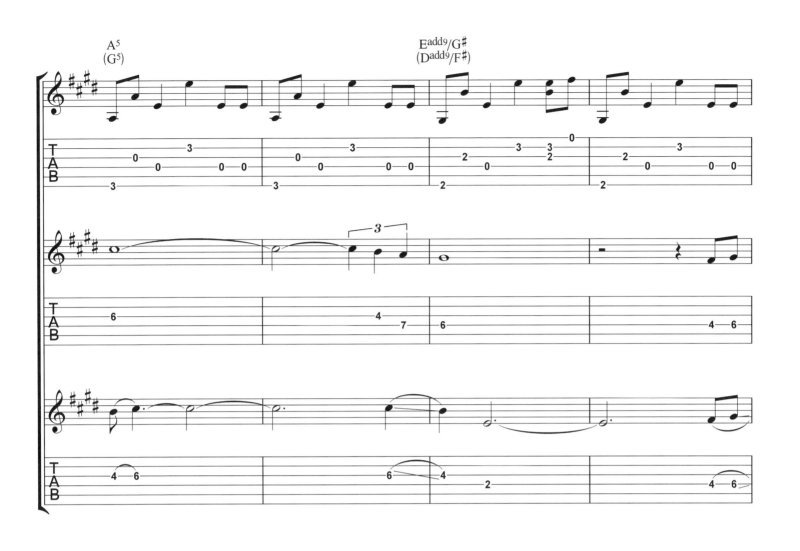

GET LUCKY

Words & Music by Mark Knopfler

Capo 4th fret

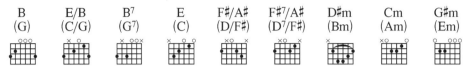

Intro

♩ = 171

Gtr. 1 (acous.)
Capo 4th fret

†Symbols in parentheses represent names with respect to capoed guitar.
Symbols above represent actual sounding chords. (Tab 0 = 4 fr.).

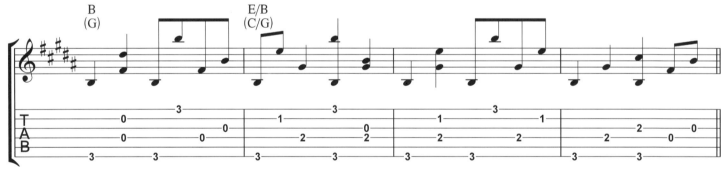

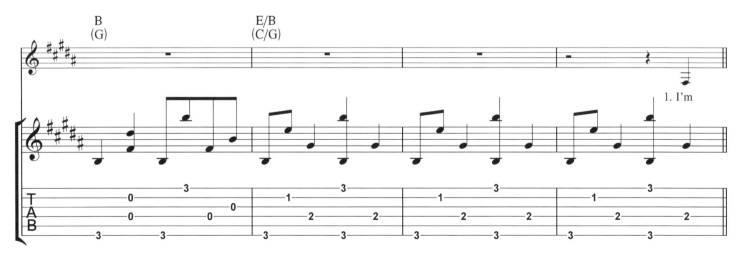

1. I'm

win some.

D.S. al Coda

Flute

Now I'm

SO FAR FROM THE CLYDE

Words & Music by Mark Knopfler

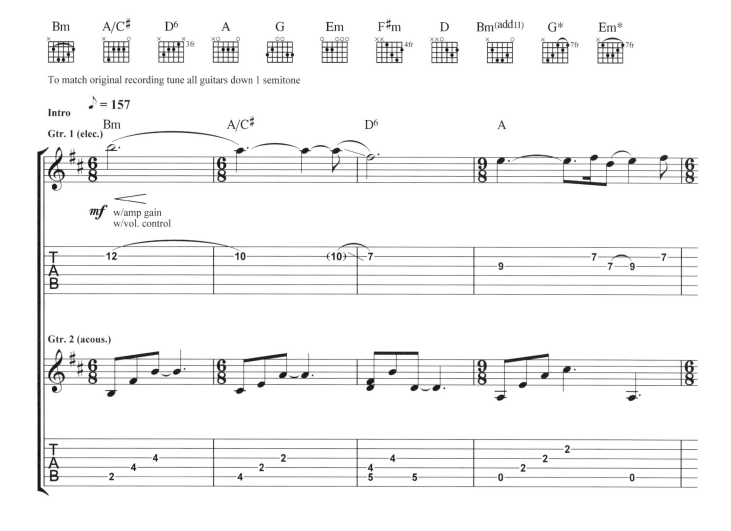

To match original recording tune all guitars down 1 semitone

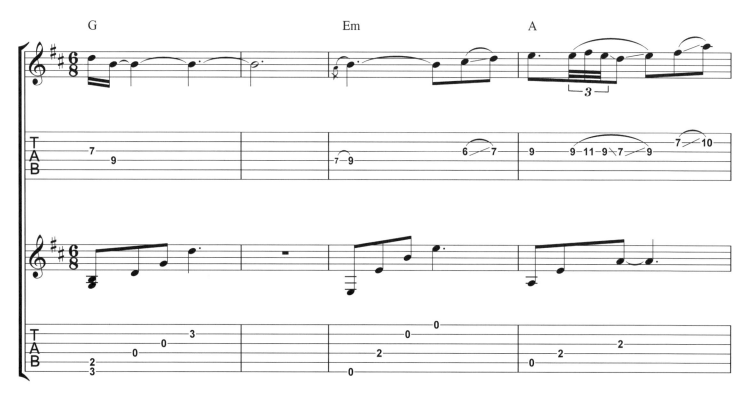

73

74

ride,   we did ride.

Whistle cue

Bm

Gtr. 2

cont. in slashes

3. As

Verse

Gtr. 2

Bm   *A*   *Bm*   *D*

if to a wave   from her bows to her   rud-der,   brave - ly   she ris - es to meet
4. La-ter the cap-tain   shakes   hands with the   hang - man   and climbs slow - ly down__ to the

Gtr. 3

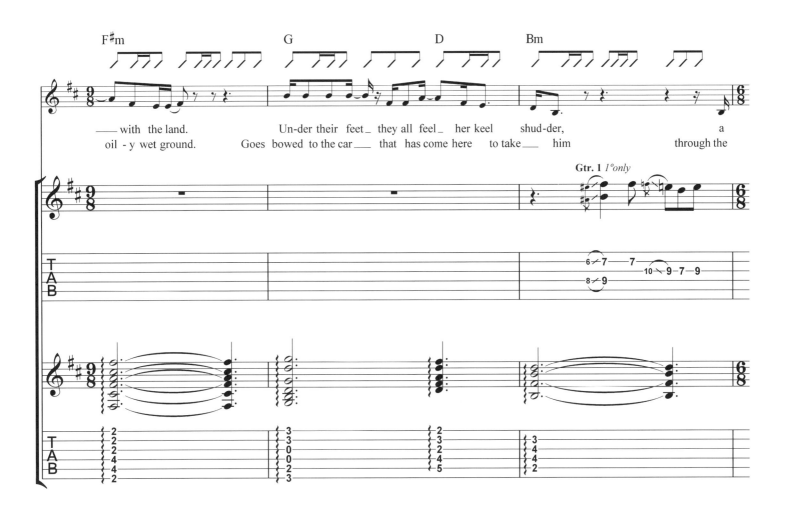

— with the land.
oil - y wet ground.
Un-der their feet_ they all feel_ her keel shud-der,
Goes bowed to the car ___ that has come here to take___ him
a
through the

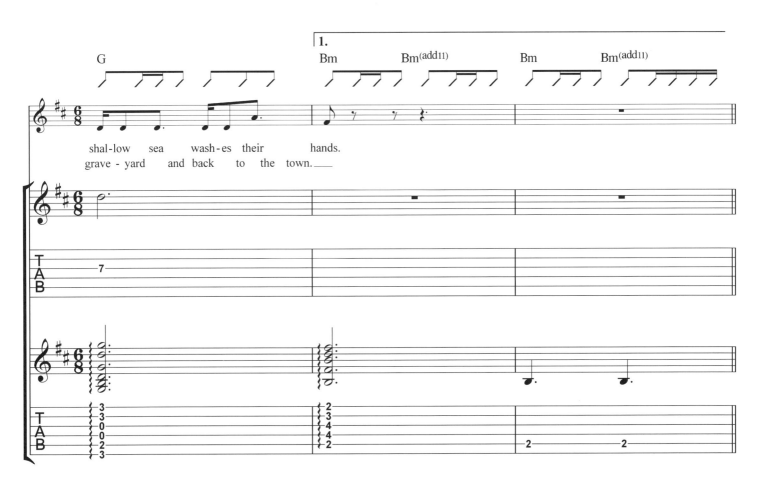

shal-low sea wash-es their hands.
grave - yard and back to the town.___

to-geth-er we'd ride,

we did ride.

D.S. al Coda

5. They

*Coda*

PIPER TO THE END

Words & Music by Mark Knopfler

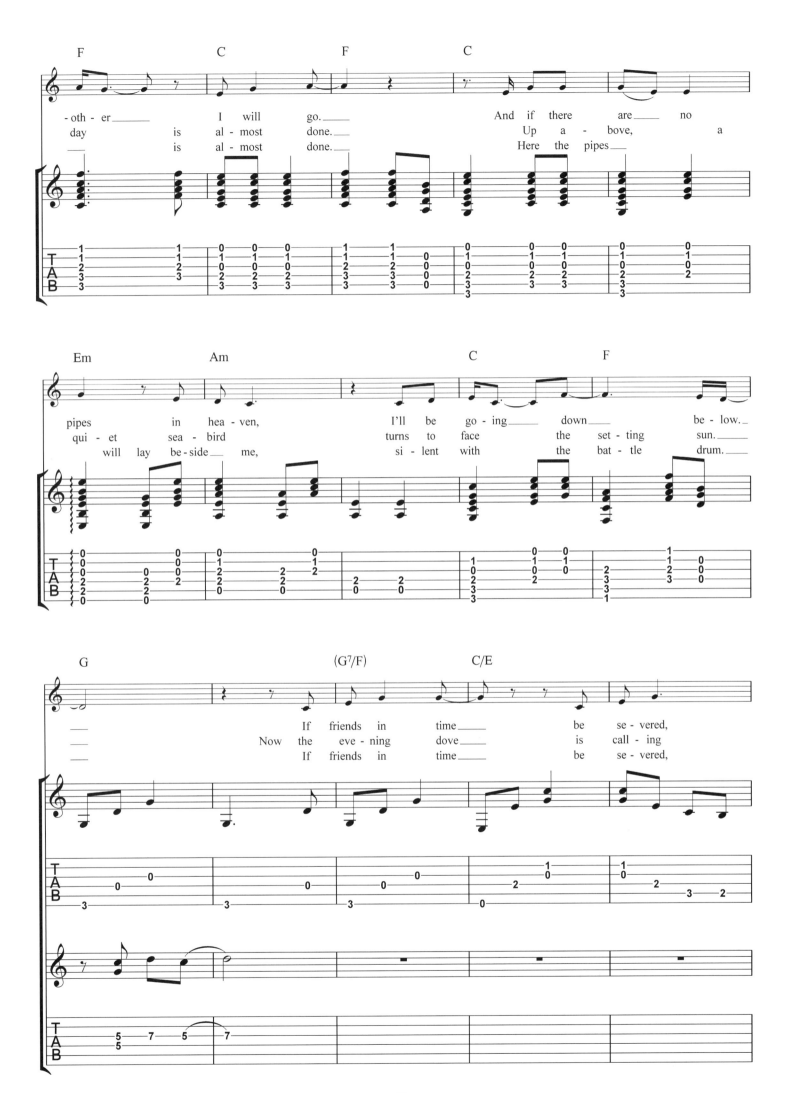

Bridge

We watched the fires ____ to - geth - er, shared our quart - ers for a while, ____ walked the dust - y roads ____ to - geth - er, came so ma - ny miles. ____

Coda

Whistle/fiddle cue

Gtr. 2

cont. ad lib. sim.

cont. ad lib. sim.

D.S. al Coda

85

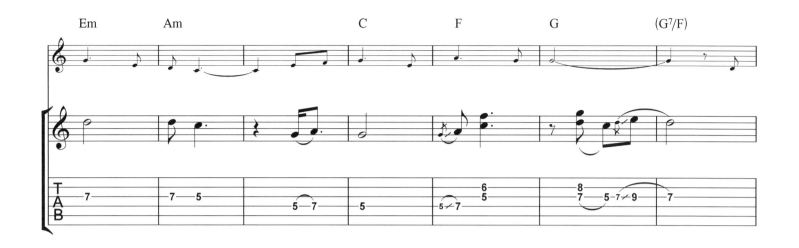

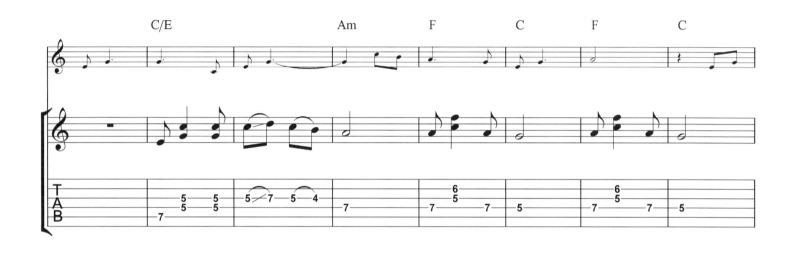

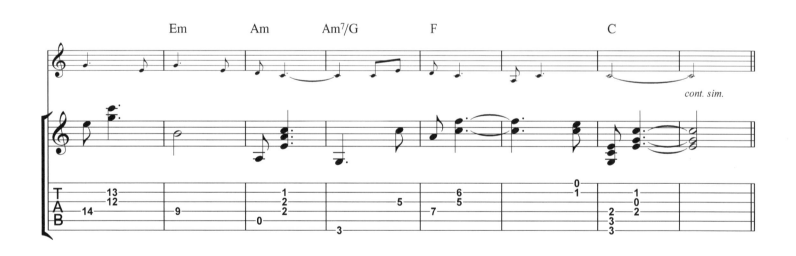

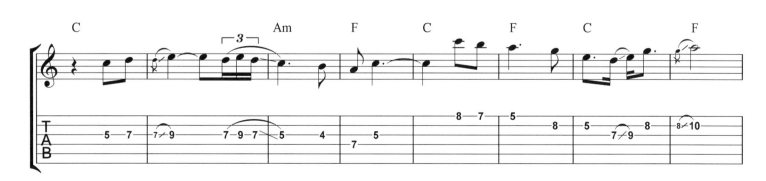

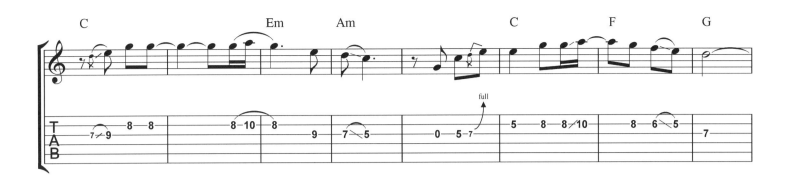

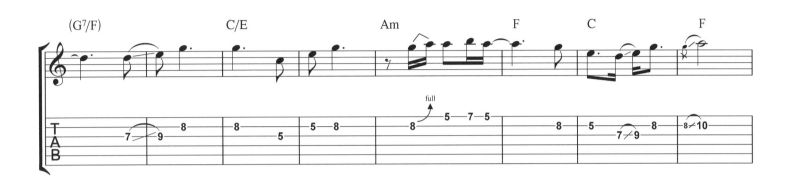

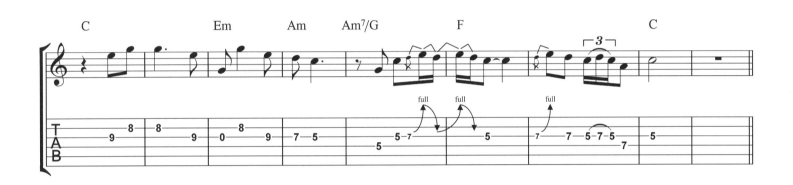

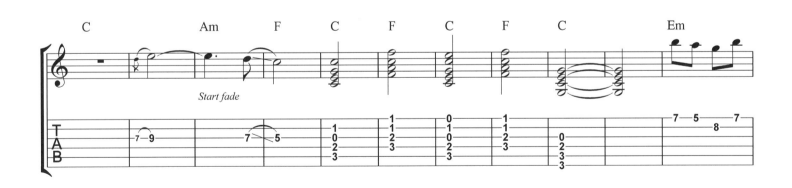

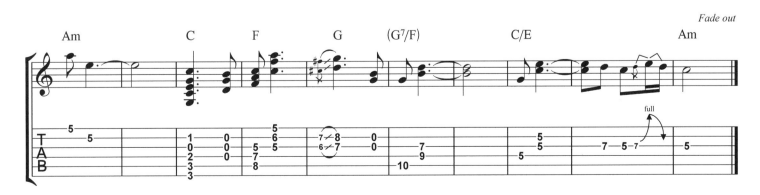

GUITAR TABLATURE EXPLAINED

Guitar music can be notated in three different ways: on a musical stave, in tablature, and in rhythm slashes.

RHYTHM SLASHES: are written above the stave. Strum chords in the rhythm indicated. Round noteheads indicate single notes.

THE MUSICAL STAVE: shows pitches and rhythms and is divided by lines into bars. Pitches are named after the first seven letters of the alphabet.

TABLATURE: graphically represents the guitar fingerboard. Each horizontal line represents a string, and each number represents a fret.

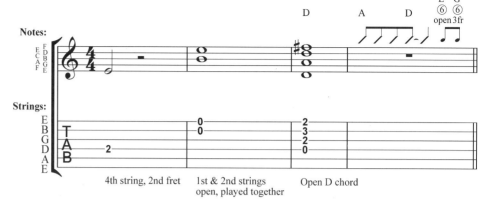

4th string, 2nd fret | 1st & 2nd strings open, played together | Open D chord

Definitions for special guitar notation

SEMI-TONE BEND: Strike the note and bend up a semi-tone (½ step).

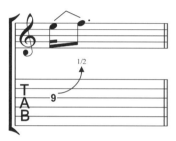

WHOLE-TONE BEND: Strike the note and bend up a whole-tone (full step).

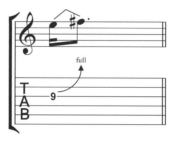

GRACE NOTE BEND: Strike the note and bend as indicated. Play the first note as quickly as possible.

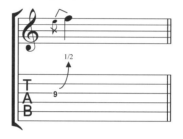

QUARTER-TONE BEND: Strike the note and bend up a ¼ step

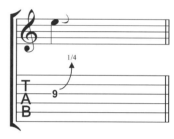

BEND & RELEASE: Strike the note and bend up as indicated, then release back to the original note.

COMPOUND BEND & RELEASE: Strike the note and bend up and down in the rhythm indicated.

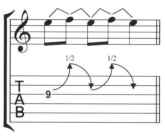

PRE-BEND: Bend the note as indicated, then strike it.

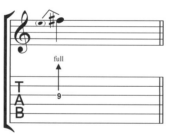

PRE-BEND & RELEASE: Bend the note as indicated. Strike it and release the note back to the original pitch.

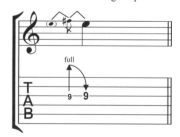

HAMMER-ON: Strike the first note with one finger, then sound the second note (on the same string) with another finger by fretting it without picking.

PULL-OFF: Place both fingers on the note to be sounded, strike the first note and without picking, pull the finger off to sound the second note.

LEGATO SLIDE (GLISS): Strike the first note and then slide the same fret-hand finger up or down to the second note. The second note is not struck.

MUFFLED STRINGS: A percussive sound is produced by laying the first hand across the string(s) without depressing, and striking them with the pick hand.

NATURAL HARMONIC: Strike the note while the fret-hand lightly touches the string directly over the fret indicated.

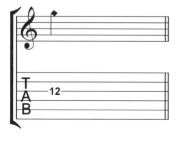

PICK SCRAPE: The edge of the pick is rubbed down (or up) the string, producing a scratchy sound.

PALM MUTING: The note is partially muted by the pick hand lightly touching the string(s) just before the bridge.

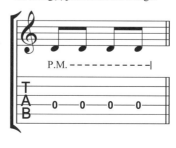

SHIFT SLIDE (GLISS & RESTRIKE) Same as legato slide, except the second note is struck.

1 2 3 4 5 6 7 8 9